The Great Little Food With Wine Cookbook

76 cooking with wine recipes.
Pairing food with wine.
How and where to buy wine.
Ordering wine in a restaurant.

by
Virginia and Robert Hoffman

The Hoffman Press
Santa Rosa, California

Typeset by Nancy LaMothe

Cover Illustration by Ellie Marshall

Quantity discounts and bulk purchases of this and other Hoffman Press books are available. Call or fax the National Sales Manager at (707) 538-5527, Fax (707) 538-7371.

Printed in the United States.

Publisher's Cataloging-in-Publication
(Provided by Quality Books, Inc.)

Hoffman, Virginia M.
     The great little food with wine cookbook : 76 cooking with wine recipes : pairing food with wine : how and where to buy wine : ordering wine in a restaurant / by Virginia and Robert Hoffman.
     p. cm.
     Includes index.
     ISBN 0-9629927-0-4
     1. Cookery (Wine) I. Hoffman, Robert P. II. Title
TX726.H64 1997   641.6'22
                              QBI97-40458

Contents

Introduction

We are not wine experts. We are two people who, probably like you, enjoy drinking wine and cooking with wine. We are fortunate enough to live in the heart of the California Wine Country. This allows us to learn firsthand how to enjoy wine to its fullest extent. We also enjoy collecting recipes created by winemakers and wine-country chefs, both amateur and professional. All of this led to our writing four cookbooks of The California Wine Country.

In this book are 76 recipes for cooking with wine. There's a chart for matching wines to your favorite foods. There are suggestions on identifying, buying and serving wine. And, there is help in deciphering wine labels and restaurant wine lists.

We hope that you have as much pleasure in using this book as we did in writing it.

Virginia and Robert Hoffman
Santa Rosa, California

How to Buy Wine

For those of us who live in or near wine-producing regions, it is quite easy to visit wineries, taste different wines, and talk to knowledgeable people about wine. For those of us who must depend upon the label on the bottle or the advice of the salesclerk, it can be a frustrating experience. It does not have to be.

We are not suggesting that you immediately enroll in a wine appreciation course, or bring along one of your friends who knows wines. While both ways of learning about wine are good, you may not have the time or the knowledgeable friends. There are some alternatives.

There are some excellent wine-buying guides that can help you. My personal favorite is Dan Berger, whose L.A. Times syndicated column appears in many newspapers nationally. He also has a weekly wine commentary, "Dan Berger's Vintage Experiences" that is faxed to consumers, retailers and wholesalers every Thursday. Another favorite of ours is Hugh Johnson, whose pocket size books are an easy way to take a wine authority shopping with you.

The wine advice in such magazines as Bon Appetit, Gourmet and Saveur is good, but the best magazines in the field are The Wine Spectator and The Wine Enthusiast.

In most states wine is sold at wine merchants and liquor stores, in supermarkets, some drug stores, and warehouse clubs.

The wine merchant can be a great help if you tell him what you are looking for. Tell him what your price range is for the occasion. If you are not impressed with his knowledge, go elsewhere.

Regrettably, many wine merchants and liquor stores are manned by personnel who are there only to run the cash register. If you are fortunate enough to find a knowledgeable wine merchant, buy your wine there. He can save you money by insuring you have good wines, rather than saving by buying at a supermarket or warehouse club.

If you have a favorite restaurant, don't hesitate to call or go in and ask the person in charge of the wine to make some suggestions. But, you don't want to buy the wine there! With rare exceptions, restaurants charge 200% to 300% more than a wine merchant's price.

The supermarkets are an easy place to shop for wine. Although the selection is usually somewhat limited and you won't find rare vintage wines, you will probably find what you want at a good price. If you need help in selecting your wine, bring a wine guide with you. The store clerks are not trained to help you and the shelf stickers are self-serving advertisements by the wineries or the store itself.

There is one exception: Some stores identify the wines by the ratings of wine experts or judges in wine competitions. These ratings can help you choose the best in each category of varietals and price ranges.

The warehouse clubs generally have the best prices for wine, but a very limited selection. As is true of supermarket shopping, don't plan on getting buying advice here.

Those of you who live in states where wine can be purchased only in state-controlled liquor stores have the smallest number of choices in wines. You may be able to buy from one of the many mail-order wine clubs and the wineries themselves. However, some states tax mail-order wine purchases, and some even prohibit the entry of wine into their states. For those of you in one of these states, our sympathy. If it is of any consolation, the wine industry is working hard to overcome these restrictions, and you can help by advising your local legislators of your desires in this matter.

The most effective way to develop a list of favorite wines is to taste them. Some wine merchants have wine tastings, usually on Saturdays. Wine bars are another good place to taste wine and get some expert advice. Wine tastings, often held as fund-raisers, present yet another opportunity.

But, the best of all is a trip to a wine-producing region. Here you can taste many different wines by many different wineries, and form your own judgements. You can get expert help from the tasting-room staff of the wineries. You can usually tour the winery and often meet the winemaker and learn first hand how your wine was made. There is no better or more enjoyable way to learn how to buy wine!

① ② ③ ④ ⑤ ⑥ ⑦ ⑧ ⑨ ⑩

AMERICAN

1993

Reserve
Estate Bottled

Ourown Vineyard
The American Valley
CHARDONNAY

Net contents 750ml 13.5% alcohol

Vinted & bottled by The American Winery, Winetown, WN USA

CONTAINS SULFITES

Understanding the Wine Label

1. THE BRAND NAME: The name, not necessarily that of the vintner, under which the wine is sold.

2. THE VINTAGE: The year the grapes were harvested, more important in regions with variable weather conditions.

3. RESERVE: Indicates superior wine due to quality of grapes, barrels, extra aging, etc.

4. ESTATE BOTTLED: The vineyards are owned or controlled by a winery, assuring quality control from vine to bottle. 95% of the wine must come from these vineyards.

5. VINEYARD NAME: Further indication of quality of wine by specifying the vineyard.

6. THE APPELLATION: Specifies the region where grapes were grown. 85% of the grapes must come from within it.

7. THE TYPE OF WINE: Identifies the varietal or class of wine, such as white, red or sparkling.

8. CONTENTS: Indicates size of bottle and percentage of alcohol below 14%, the US legal limit.

9. NAME & ADDRESS OF BOTTLER

10. SULFITE STATEMENT: Most wines contain sulfur dioxide, an anti-bacterial agent.

Soups

Champagne Onion Soup

This is a really special onion soup, not like anything you've ever tasted.

1 cube butter
4 cups thinly sliced onions
2 cloves garlic, chopped
4 cups chicken broth
1 ½ cups Champagne (Brut)
Salt and pepper
4 tablespoons Cognac
2 egg yolks
Croutons
Swiss cheese, grated

Melt the butter and sauté onions and garlic until soft and yellow, but not brown. Pour into kettle, add broth and Champagne. Simmer for one hour. Add salt and pepper to taste, and Cognac.

Beat egg yolks until pale and soft. Add 2 to 3 ounces of soup to the egg yolks to dilute them so they will be warmed, but will not cook when put into soup. Pour back into the soup. Stir well. Keep hot, but not boiling.

To serve, float croutons on top of the soup. Sprinkle generously with cheese. Serves 6.

Serve with Champagne (Brut).

The secret to opening a bottle of Champagne easily is to wrap a towel around the top of the bottle, after you've removed the foil and wire. Hold the cork firmly in one hand, and twist the bottle, not the cork. This will open it easily, safely, and with a minimum loss of the wine.

Onion Soup Parmesan

12 medium onions, sliced thin
6 tablespoons butter
2 tablespoons flour
4 cups beef stock
1 cup Burgundy wine
Salt
30 to 40 croutons
Grated Parmesan cheese

Sauté sliced onions in butter until golden brown. Add flour and stir until smooth. Add beef stock and wine. Simmer about 30 minutes. Add salt to taste and stir. Pour into soup casseroles.

Place 4 to 5 croutons on top of each casserole and sprinkle with Parmesan cheese. Place casseroles in 400 degree oven until cheese melts. Serves 8.

Serve with Burgundy or Pinot Noir.

Cream of Avocado Soup

Personally, we like this soup served cold for an elegant summer picnic.

4 large, ripe avocados
3 cups chicken broth
½ teaspoon salt
Pinch of white pepper
½ teaspoon Worcestershire sauce
½ cup white wine
1 cup light cream
½ cup heavy cream, whipped
Nutmeg

Peel, pit and cube avocados, then purée in blender.

In a saucepan, mix avocado purée, chicken broth, salt, pepper and Worcestershire sauce. Heat to boiling point, stirring occasionally. Add wine. Stir in light cream. Cover and simmer 10 minutes.

Serve soup hot; garnish each bowl with a dollop of whipped cream and a sprinkling of nutmeg.   Serves 6.

Serve with Sauvignon Blanc or Reisling.

Sherry Mushroom Soup

In a hurry? Eliminate the first 5 ingredients, and substitute a can of condensed mushroom soup.

1 pound fresh mushrooms, sliced
1 large onion, thinly sliced
2 tablespoons butter or margarine
2 tablespoons flour
4 cups beef broth
¾ cup Sherry
6 slices French bread, toasted
½ cup shredded Gruyere cheese

In a 4-quart saucepan, cook mushrooms and onion in butter until onion is soft. Stir in flour. Cook, stirring for 1 to 2 minutes. Add broth. Simmer, covered, for 10 minutes. Stir in Sherry.

Preheat broiler. Place toasted bread on a baking sheet and sprinkle with cheese. Broil until cheese is melted. Divide soup evenly into 6 serving bowls. Float a piece of cheese toast in each bowl.   Serves 6.

Serve with Pinot Noir or Merlot.

Garlic Soup

3 cloves garlic, minced
2 tablespoons olive oil
2 ounces prosciutto (ham), chopped (about 4
  tablespoons)
3 cups toasted bread cubes
1 tablespoon paprika
4 cups chicken broth
1 cup Sauvignon Blanc wine

Sauté garlic in olive oil until golden brown. Add prosciutto and sauté until lightly browned. Add bread cubes and paprika. Sauté 3 minutes. Add broth and wine and heat through.

Serve immediately.   Serves 4 to 6.

Serve with Sauvignon Blanc or Chardonnay.

Cauliflower Soup

Ideal for that "Big Game" buffet or a mid-winter country meal.

**4 slices Italian or French bread, crusts removed and
  cubed
½ cup plus 2 tablespoons butter
4 cups fresh cauliflower florets
4 large potatoes, peeled and cubed
1 teaspoon salt
6 cups milk
¼ cup white wine
Salt and pepper
Paprika**

Fry bread cubes in ½ cup of the butter until crisp and golden brown. Place on absorbent paper towel; wrap in foil. Keep warm until serving time.

Combine cauliflower, potatoes, salt and 4 cups of the milk in a 5-quart saucepan. Bring to a boil; reduce heat to low. Cover; simmer for 30 minutes or until vegetables are fork tender. Remove from heat.

Mash mixture; vegetables will be lumpy. Stir in remaining milk and butter. Add wine and blend. Adjust flavor with salt and pepper. Bring to a boil.

Ladle into heated bowls. Garnish with fried bread cubes; sprinkle with paprika.   Serves 10.

Serve with a Sauvignon Blanc or Reisling.

Shrimp Bisque

A New Orleans beginning for your meal, or serve with French bread and a salad.

1 ½ pounds shrimp, peeled and deveined
4 cups water
4 to 5 celery leaves
1 tablespoon salt
1 medium onion, minced
7 tablespoons butter
8 tablespoons flour
2 cups chicken broth
1 cup cream
⅔ cup Sherry

Cook shrimp in 4 cups boiling water to which the celery leaves and salt have been added. Boil for 5 minutes. Drain shrimp and reserve liquid, removing celery leaves. Mince the shrimp very fine.

In a saucepan, sauté onion in butter. When onion is soft, add flour. Blend well and add chicken broth. Stir until thick; add the reserved shrimp liquid. Simmer for 5 minutes, then add minced shrimp and the cream. Add Sherry just before serving.   Serves 6.

Serve with Pinot Gris or Sémillon.

Shiitake Mushroom Bisque
A personal favorite.

3 cups low-sodium chicken stock
1 ounce dried porcini mushrooms
¼ cup butter
2 celery stalks, minced
½ cup minced onion
2 garlic cloves, minced
½ pound fresh shiitake mushrooms, stemmed and
  sliced
2 tablespoons all-purpose flour
½ teaspoon dried oregano
⅛ teaspoon dried crushed red pepper
1 cup half-and-half
½ cup Sherry Fino
Salt and pepper

Bring stock to a simmer in heavy, medium saucepan. Add porcini mushrooms. Remove from heat. Cover and let steep for 30 minutes. Remove porcini mushrooms and chop; reserve stock.

Melt butter in heavy saucepan over medium heat. Add celery, onion and garlic and sauté until onion is tender, about 8 minutes. Add the mushrooms and sauté 3 minutes. Add flour, oregano and dried red pepper. Sauté 3 minutes.

Gradually whisk in reserved stock and half-and-half. Bring to a boil. Reduce heat and simmer until slightly thickened, about 10 minutes. Add Sherry and simmer 5 minutes. Season to taste with salt and pepper.   Serves 4.

Serve with a Sauvignon Blanc or Chenin Blanc.

Tomato Soup with Sherry

A nice soup for a "soup-n-sandwich" luncheon or a formal dinner party.

1 medium onion, chopped
1 medium carrot, coarsely shredded
3 tablespoons butter or margarine
¼ cup all-purpose flour
1 teaspoon salt
½ teaspoon ground nutmeg
4 cups canned tomato juice
2 cups beef broth
½ cup dry Sherry
1 tablespoon minced fresh parsley
1 tablespoon honey

In a saucepan, cook onion and carrot in butter until tender, but not brown. Stir in flour, salt and nutmeg.

Add tomato juice and beef broth. Cook and stir until bubbling and slightly thickened. Add Sherry, parsley and honey. Simmer for an additional 5 to 10 minutes. Serves 6.

Serve with Chardonnay or Chenin Blanc.

Cream of Broccoli Soup

Another soup which we think is best when served cold, but is delicious either way.

4 cups chopped fresh broccoli
½ cup chopped onion
3 cups chicken stock
½ teaspoon thyme
½ clove garlic, minced
½ cup Fumé Blanc wine
4 tablespoons butter
¼ cup unsifted flour
⅛ teaspoon pepper
2 cups light cream

In a large saucepan, combine the broccoli, onion, chicken stock, thyme and garlic. Bring to a boil, reduce heat, cover, and simmer for 15 minutes or until broccoli is tender.

Using ⅓ of the mixture at a time, blend until smooth in a blender or food processor. Return the mixture to the saucepan and add the wine. Set aside.

Melt the butter in a medium saucepan over low heat. Stir in the flour and pepper until smooth. Stir in cream. Cook until mixture is thickened, then add it to the broccoli mixture. Heat the combined mixture together until hot; do not boil.

Serve hot or cold.   Serves 6.

Serve this flavorsome soup with Fumé Blanc or Sauvignon Blanc.

Mushroom Bisque with Sherry

1 pound fresh mushrooms
3 tablespoons butter
4 tablespoons flour
Salt and pepper
4 cups chicken stock
1 cup Sherry
1 cup heavy cream
Nutmeg

Clean and slice the mushrooms. Place in heavy skillet with no fat nor liquid. Cover and place over medium heat until the mushrooms are almost completely dry and begin to stick to the pan. Stir in butter.

When butter is melted, stir in flour and continue to cook, stirring constantly, for about 5 minutes. Add salt and pepper to taste. Blend in chicken stock with a wire whisk until stock is slightly thickened. Cool slightly.

Blend in Sherry and cream. Reheat, but do not boil. Float nutmeg on top of each bowl before serving. Serves 6 to 8.

Serve with Chardonnay or Reisling.

Black Bean Chili

If you're looking for an après ski recipe, this is it.

2 cups diced bacon
1 onion, diced small
1 clove garlic, minced
1 pound sirloin steak, cut into ¼-inch strips
3 cups black beans
1 cup red wine
2 whole tomatoes, peeled and chopped
10 cups beef stock
3 bay leaves
1 tablespoon cumin
2 tablespoons chili powder
¼ teaspoon cayenne pepper
¼ cup chopped fresh cilantro
6 tablespoons sour cream

Sauté bacon until crisp. Add onion and garlic; sauté until brown. Add sirloin and sauté until brown.

Add remaining ingredients except cilantro and sour cream. Cook for 2 to 2 ½ hours. While cooking, adjust liquid with more stock and wine, if necessary. Remove bay leaves.

Serve with cilantro and sour cream.   Serves 6 to 8.

Serve with a Barbera or Pinot Noir.

Pastas &
Grains

Mushroom Turkey Fettuccine
A neighbor, who owns a small Italian family winery, serves this to VIP visitors.

4 turkey fillets (approximately 1 ¼ pounds total)
3 tablespoons butter
1 medium onion, minced
2 cups Champagne
2 cups whipping cream
½ pound mushrooms, sliced
2 tablespoons capers
2 tablespoons chopped chives
Salt and pepper
8 ounces fettuccine pasta, cooked according to
  package directions
Minced parsley for garnish

Brown turkey fillets in butter 3 to 4 minutes on each side. Add onions and Champagne; cover and simmer 10 minutes. Remove fillets and keep warm.

Increase heat to high and let Champagne reduce by half. Add cream and remaining ingredients except pasta; simmer 10 to 15 minutes until slightly thickened. Slice fillets; serve on bed of pasta dividing turkey slices among plates. Top with sauce and minced parsley.   Serves 6.

Champagne, Sémillon or Reisling will go well with this rich pasta dish.

Fettuccine with a Sherried Mushroom Sauce

5 tablespoons butter
1 ½ cup chopped onions
1 ¼ pounds mushrooms, sliced
1 ¼ cups cream
¼ cup dry Sherry
1 tablespoon chopped fresh thyme
Salt and pepper
12 ounces fettuccine
¼ cup minced fresh parsley
Freshly grated Parmesan cheese

Melt butter in heavy skillet over medium-high heat. Add onions and sauté until they begin to brown, about 8 minutes. Add mushrooms and sauté until light brown, about 6 minutes.

Add cream, Sherry and thyme. Cook until reduced to sauce consistency, stirring occasionally, for 5 minutes. Season to taste with salt and pepper. Set aside.

Cook pasta in large pot of boiling salted water until just tender, but still firm to bite. Drain. Transfer pasta to large bowl. Bring sauce to simmer. Pour sauce over pasta; toss well. Sprinkle with parsley and Parmesan cheese.

Serves 4.

Serve with Chardonnay, Sémillon or Reisling.

Penne Pasta Tomato Beef

If you don't have penne pasta, any large tube pasta will do quite well.

1 pound lean ground beef
2 cloves garlic, minced
1 medium onion, chopped
½ cup chopped red bell pepper
1 ½ cups sliced mushrooms
1 can (16 ounces) Italian-style stewed tomatoes
1 cup red wine
1 teaspoon thyme
½ teaspoon salt
¼ teaspoon black pepper
1 teaspoon oregano
2 tablespoons chopped fresh basil
¾ pound penne pasta, cooked according to package
  directions

Brown beef. Add garlic, onion and pepper. Cook until slightly browned. Add mushrooms. Sauté for several minutes before adding tomatoes and wine.

Add thyme, salt, pepper and oregano. Simmer uncovered for 30 minutes. Add more wine as sauce thickens, if necessary. Just before serving, add fresh chopped basil.

Serve hot over pasta.   Serves 6.

Serve with a Merlot, Barbera or Pinot Noir.

Chicken Pappardelle

3 tablespoons extra virgin olive oil
6 tablespoons sweet butter
1 stalk celery, minced
1 large onion, minced
1 large carrot, minced
4 ounces prosciutto, chopped
½ teaspoon chopped fresh sage
3 boneless, skinless chicken breasts, halved
1 cup Merlot wine
1 can (16 ounces) Italian plum tomatoes
½ teaspoon dried oregano
Pinch of salt
Pinch of lemon pepper
1 teaspoon sugar
1 pound fresh pappardelle pasta (a wide noodle-like
  pasta with a fluted edge)

To make the sauce, heat the oil and butter in a large deep pan. Add the celery, onion, carrot, prosciutto and sage. After 3 minutes, add the chicken breasts and cook for 5 minutes, stirring. Pour in the wine. When the wine is nearly evaporated, add the tomatoes, oregano, salt, pepper and sugar. Cook over low heat for 45 minutes. If sauce is too thick, add more wine.

When sauce is almost done, cook the pappardelle pasta according to package directions (al dente). Drain; transfer to a large serving bowl. Remove chicken pieces from sauce. Cut chicken into chunks and set aside. Mix the pasta with the sauce, and top with pieces of chicken.   Serves 6.

Serve with Merlot or Pinot Noir.

Easy Noodles Romanoff

1 package (8 ounces) wide egg noodles
2 tablespoons margarine or butter
2 cups sour cream
½ cup grated Parmesan cheese
¼ cup Dry Vermouth
1 tablespoon chopped fresh chives
½ teaspoon salt
⅛ teaspoon pepper
1 large clove garlic, minced

Cook noodles as directed on package; drain. Stir margarine into hot noodles. Mix sour cream, ¼ cup of the cheese, Vermouth, chives, salt, pepper and garlic.

Stir sour cream mixture into noodles. Place on warm platter. Sprinkle with the remaining ¼ cup of cheese.   Serves 6.

Serve with Chardonnay, Sémillon or Reisling.

If you have a bottle of wine whose cork is so tight it simply won't come out, wrap a cloth that has been immersed in near-boiling water around the neck of the bottle. It will expand the glass enough to ease the removal of the cork with a corkscrew.

Tomato-Crabmeat Vermicelli

A very unusual and satisfying pasta dish.

1 tablespoon olive oil
1 large white onion, chopped
4 stalks celery, chopped fine
3 tablespoons chopped fresh parsley
1 clove garlic, minced
1 tablespoon chopped fresh basil
1 tablespoon chopped fresh oregano
1 can (16 ounces) tomatoes
1 can (6 ounces) tomato paste
½ cup water
1 cup white wine
1 pound crabmeat, chopped
½ pound vermicelli pasta
1 cup grated Parmesan cheese

Heat oil in skillet; add onion and celery and brown slightly, sautéing until soft. Add parsley, garlic, herbs, tomatoes, tomato paste, water and wine. Simmer for 30 minutes. Add crabmeat and heat.

Cook pasta according to package instructions.

For each portion, serve pasta topped with crabmeat sauce and a generous sprinkling of cheese.   Serves 6.

Serve with Chardonnay or Sémillon.

Baked Beef and Macaroni Casserole
This is truly a meal unto itself — it is very rich.

1 ½ pounds ground beef
1 medium onion, minced
1 clove garlic, minced
¼ cup olive oil
2 cans (8 ounces each) tomato sauce
4 ripe tomatoes, chopped
1 cup red wine
1 ½ teaspoons dried oregano
1 ½ teaspoons dried basil
2 tablespoons chopped fresh parsley
1 tablespoon brown sugar
¼ teaspoon salt
¼ teaspoon black pepper
¾ pound dry macaroni
1 ½ cups grated Cheddar cheese (medium-sharp)

Sauté beef, onion and garlic in heated olive oil. Add tomato sauce, tomatoes, wine, herbs, parsley, sugar, salt and pepper. Simmer, covered, for 30 minutes stirring occasionally.

Cook macaroni according to package directions; drain. Add macaroni and ½ cup of the cheese to the sauce. Turn into a 3-quart casserole; sprinkle with the remaining cup of cheese. Cover and bake in a 325 degree oven for 45 minutes. Uncover and bake 20 minutes longer.   Serves 6.

Serve with Burgundy, Barbera or Merlot.

Crab à la King Fettuccine

2 tablespoons butter
1 tablespoon minced celery
1 tablespoon flour
½ teaspoon salt
¼ teaspoon freshly ground pepper
1 teaspoon chopped fresh parsley
1 cup heavy cream
2 hard-boiled eggs, finely diced
1 tablespoon finely chopped chives
2 cups chopped crabmeat
¼ cup dry Sherry
¾ pound fettuccine, cooked according to package
  directions
Paprika
Chopped parsley for garnish

Slowly melt the butter over low heat in a heavy skillet. Add the celery and cook, stirring frequently, for 5 minutes. Add the flour a little at a time, stirring constantly, to form a smooth mixture. Add the salt, pepper and parsley. Mix throughly.

Blend in the cream. Cook on low heat until mixture begins to thicken, about 6 to 8 minutes. Stir frequently. Add the eggs, chives and crabmeat. Cook an additional minute to heat thoroughly, stirring constantly. Add the Sherry and stir gently.

Serve immediately over hot fettuccine. Sprinkle with paprika and chopped parsley.   Serves 4.

Serve with Chardonnay or Sauvignon Blanc.

Pasta Prosciutto

¼ pound lean, thick-sliced prosciutto, cubed
2 tablespoons olive oil
1 cup coarsely chopped onion
¾ cup red wine
1 clove garlic, minced
4 to 5 medium ripe tomatoes, peeled and cut into
  chunks
1 medium red bell pepper, seeded and finely chopped
2 tablespoons chopped fresh basil
Salt
¾ pound thin spaghetti, cooked according to package
  directions and drained
¾ cup grated Parmesan cheese

Sauté prosciutto until golden, but not entirely crisp. Remove from pan and drain, leaving 2 tablespoons of the drippings. Add olive oil, onion and ¼ cup of the wine. Simmer for 3 minutes. Add remaining wine, garlic and tomatoes. Bring to a simmer. Add prosciutto and red pepper. Cook for 3 minutes. Add basil; season with salt to taste.

Cook about 5 minutes more until slightly blended. Tomatoes should remain in chunks and sauce should be a bit liquid. pour sauce over spaghetti, toss with Parmesan cheese.

Serves 4 to 6.

Serve with Merlot, Barbera or Pinot Noir.

Lemon Capers Fettuccine

1 package (8 ounces) fettuccine pasta
2 tablespoons freshly grated lemon zest
2 cloves garlic, minced
½ cup olive oil
½ cup dry white wine
2 tablespoons capers
1 tablespoon lemon juice
2 tablespoons chopped fresh basil
½ teaspoon salt
½ teaspoon freshly ground pepper
2 tablespoons chopped fresh parsley
¾ cup grated Parmesan cheese

Cook pasta, as directed on package, in boiling water to which you have added lemon zest. Drain and set aside.

Cook garlic in olive oil in a 1-quart saucepan over medium heat until garlic is golden. Stir in wine, capers, lemon juice, basil, salt and pepper. Heat just until hot. Toss with hot pasta. Sprinkle with parsley. Serve with grated Parmesan cheese.   Serves 4 to 6.

Serve with a Fumé Blanc, Sémillon or Chenin Blanc.

Risotto Milanese

Arborio rice is the key to this recipe. No other rice will do.

1 ½ cups chopped onions
½ cup olive oil
1 ½ cups arborio rice
16 saffron threads
2 cups white wine
7 cups chicken stock
Pinch of salt and pepper
2 tablespoons butter
Pinch of nutmeg
¼ cup grated Parmesan cheese

Cook the onions in oil over low heat until transparent, but not browned. Add rice and cook for 2 minutes. Add saffron and wine. Reduce by one half over medium heat, about 15 minutes.

Stirring constantly, add ½ cup stock at a time until liquid is absorbed. Cook 15 to 18 minutes until al dente. Adjust seasoning to taste with salt and pepper. Remove from heat and vigorously stir in butter, nutmeg and cheese. Serve hot.
Serves 4.

Serve with a Sauvignon Blanc, Chardonnay or Reisling.

Lemon Risotto
The lemon juice and zest add a whole new dimension to risotto.

2 tablespoons olive oil
1 cup chopped onion
2 cups arborio rice
1 cup Sémillon wine
5 tablespoons fresh lemon juice
3 teaspoons grated lemon peel
4 cups canned chicken broth
2 tablespoons butter
½ cup freshly grated Parmesan cheese
Salt and pepper
2 tablespoons chopped Italian parsley

Heat oil in heavy saucepan over medium heat. Add onion and sauté until tender, about 3 minutes. Add rice, stir 1 minute. Add wine, lemon juice and lemon peel. Reduce heat; simmer until liquid is absorbed.

Add chicken broth 1 cup at a time, allowing liquid to absorb each time. Continue this method, stirring frequently, for about 25 minutes until rice is just tender but still firm to the bite, and risotto mixture is creamy.

Remove risotto from heat. Add butter and cheese; stir until melted. Season with salt and pepper. Garnish with parsley.
Serves 6 to 8.

Serve with a Sémillon, Reisling or Chardonnay.

Mediterranean Pilaf

An ideal accompaniment to lamb chops, leg of lamb or lamb shanks.

½ cup olive oil
1 cup pearl barley
¾ cup bulgur wheat
½ pound fresh mushrooms, sliced
2 medium onions, sliced thin
1 cup dry white wine
1 cup chicken broth
⅛ teaspoon pepper
2 bay leaves
Chopped fresh parsley for garnish

In a frying pan, heat olive oil over medium heat. Add barley, wheat, mushrooms and onions. Sauté, stirring constantly until onions are limp and clear. Reduce heat, if necessary, to prevent grains from burning.

Transfer mixture to a 2 ½-quart casserole. Pour in the wine and broth; add pepper and stir. Place bay leaves in casserole. Cover casserole and bake in a preheated 325 degree oven for 1 hour or until there is no free-flowing liquid. Remove bay leaves. Sprinkle with chopped parsley.

Serves 6.

Try a Reisling or Zinfandel.

Meats

Burgundy Beef Ragout

The Burgundy region of France is the birthplace of this recipe.

3 pounds beef sirloin, cut into 2-inch cubes
¼ cup all-purpose flour
2 teaspoons salt
¼ teaspoon pepper
¼ cup olive oil
¾ cup minced scallions, with some tops
1 large clove garlic, crushed
2 cups dry red wine
2 sprigs parsley
1 bay leaf
1 teaspoon dried thyme
½ pound fresh mushrooms, cleaned and halved
1 can (16 ounces) small white onions, drained

Wipe beef cubes dry with paper towel. Dredge with flour which has been seasoned with salt and pepper. In a large saucepan, brown on all sides in heated olive oil. Remove to a plate.

To the same saucepan, add scallions and garlic; sauté 1 minute. Add wine, parsley, bay leaf and thyme. Return beef to pan; mix well. Bring to a boil and lower heat. Cook slowly, covered, for about 1 ½ hours until beef is tender.

Add mushrooms and onions during last 10 minutes of cooking. Remove and discard parsley and bay leaf.

Serves 8.

Serve with Barbera or a Cabernet Sauvignon.

Brandied Beef in a Cream Sauce
That little bit of Brandy does a great job of blending all the flavors together.

2 tablespoons olive oil
1 ½ pounds beef fillet, cut into long, thin strips
2 tablespoons butter
½ cup finely chopped onion
½ pound mushrooms, sliced (approximately 2 cups)
4 tablespoons Brandy
4 tablespoons Hungarian paprika
½ cup heavy cream
½ cup sour cream
Salt and freshly ground pepper

In a large, heavy skillet, heat the oil over high heat. Add the beef and sear quickly. It should be medium-rare in the center. Remove to a warm platter.

In another skillet, heat the butter over medium-high heat and sauté onions until they are soft. Add mushrooms and cook quickly for 3 to 4 minutes. Lower heat to medium. Add the Brandy and paprika to the mushrooms; stir. Cook for 1 minute. Add heavy cream and sour cream and stir until heated. Do not allow sauce to boil.

Return beef to sauce and heat. Again, do not allow sauce to boil. Season to taste with salt and pepper.   Serves 4.

Serve with a Pinot Noir or Merlot.

Sauerbraten
The classic German recipe.

2 teaspoons salt
½ teaspoon freshly ground pepper
4 pounds beef round or chuck, suitable for pot roast
½ cup finely sliced onion
½ cup red wine vinegar
1 ½ cups Merlot wine
½ cup cold water
2 tablespoons butter, melted
12 gingersnap cookies, crumbled
1 teaspoon sugar
1 cup hot water

Rub salt and pepper into beef, and place in roasting pan with onion, vinegar, ½ cup of the wine, and the cold water. Cover pan and roast in oven at 350 degrees for 4 hours, basting frequently.

When meat is done, make the gravy. Mix together the butter, gingersnaps and sugar. Add hot water and the remaining wine. Cook for 5 minutes or until thickened. Strain the wine and cooking juices from the roast and add to the gravy. Stir until smooth.

To serve, place slices on platter or plates. Pour gravy over, or serve the gravy separately in a gravy boat.   Serves 6.

We suggest you serve a Merlot or Pinot Noir with this dish.

Beef Stroganoff
Better than the original Russian recipe.

2 pounds sirloin or fillet beef
½ teaspoon salt
½ teaspoon pepper
2 tablespoons flour
5 tablespoons butter
2 cups beef stock
½ cup Cabernet Sauvignon wine
3 tablespoons sour cream
2 tablespoons tomato paste
3 tablespoons finely grated onion

Cut beef into thin strips and sprinkle with salt and pepper. Set aside.

In a saucepan, blend flour with 2 tablespoons of the butter. Gradually stir in beef stock and wine, cooking until mixture thickens. Add sour cream alternately with tomato paste, stirring constantly. Simmer, but do not boil.

In a skillet, sauté beef strips and the onion in the remaining 3 tablespoons butter. Add to sauce, mixing thoroughly. Simmer for 3 to 5 minutes.

May be served as is, or over noodles.   Serves 6.

Cabernet Sauvignon or Pinot Noir is suggested to accompany this dish.

Burgundy Beef Stir-Fry

A very easy, fast recipe for an Asian-flavored entrée.

½ cup Burgundy wine
2 tablespoons teriyaki sauce
¾ pound sliced lean sirloin, cut into ½-inch strips
1 tablespoon cornstarch
2 tablespoons olive oil
1 package (6 ounces) frozen pea pods, thawed
1 cup sliced fresh mushrooms
Pepper and salt

In a small bowl, combine wine and teriyaki sauce. Add meat; stir to coat. Cover. Marinate at least one hour, stirring occasionally. Stir in cornstarch.

In large skillet, heat oil. Stir-fry meat and marinade in hot oil until sauce thickens. Add pea pods and mushrooms.

Continue cooking over high heat, stirring constantly for 2 to 3 minutes or until heated through. Season with pepper. Add salt if desired. Serve hot over rice. Serves 2.

Serve with Burgundy, Pinot Noir or Merlot.

Cooking rice? Before you add your liquid, stir in a little white wine or sherry and melted butter into the uncooked rice. They bring a whole new taste to rice!

Beef and Mushrooms in Red Wine
A classic French wine region ragout.

3 tablespoons olive oil
2 pounds lean beef stew meat, cut into 1-inch cubes
2 cloves garlic, peeled and sliced
2 cups Pinot Noir wine
½ cup beef stock
1 pound mushrooms, sliced
1 bay leaf
1 teaspoon thyme
Salt and pepper

Heat oil in large skillet and brown the meat. Remove meat to a casserole. Add the garlic to the skillet and sauté for 1 minute. Add 1 cup of the wine, scraping brown bits from the bottom of the skillet. Pour mixture over meat and add the rest of the wine. Cover casserole and marinate overnight.

The next day, add the remaining ingredients to the casserole, cover and place in a 325 degree oven for 2 ½ hours. Remove bay leaf. Thicken with a roux (a mixture of butter and flour) if desired. Serve with noodles or rice.
Serves 4 to 6.

Serve with a Pinot Noir, Cabernet Sauvignon or Merlot.

Brandy may be used in place of wine in many recipes, but remember that it is more highly concentrated and has a higher alcohol content. Use less, and cook it at a lower heat and longer to dispel the alcohol, particularly when making gravy.

Greek Beef Stifado
A superb wine-flavored stew.

**4 pounds boneless beef chuck or stew meat, cut into 1
 ½-inch cubes**
⅔ cup olive oil
4 pounds small white onions, peeled
1 can (6 ounces) tomato paste
1 ½ cups dry red wine
3 to 4 cloves garlic, peeled and halved
1 cinnamon stick, or 2 teaspoons ground cinnamon
6 whole cloves
2 bay leaves
1 tablespoon salt
¾ teaspoon pepper

Wipe beef cubes dry. Heat ½ cup of the oil in a large kettle
and brown the beef cubes, several at a time. Remove kettle
from heat and set aside. Sauté onions in the remaining oil in
a large skillet until golden on all sides.

Spoon onions with drippings over beef cubes. Combine
tomato paste and red wine. Pour over beef and onions. Add
remaining ingredients.

Cook very slowly, tightly covered, for about 2 hours until
beef is tender. Add a little wine if needed. The final sauce
should be quite thick and will be better if cooked very slowly.
Discard garlic, cinnamon sticks, cloves and bay leaves
before serving.   Serves 12.

Serve with Cabernet Sauvignon or Merlot.

Lamb Chops with Sun-Dried Tomatoes and Basil

Lamb chops rise to a new heighth with this recipe.

8 double lamb chops
2 tablespoons prepared mustard
Salt and freshly ground pepper
4 tablespoons butter
½ cup chopped onions
¼ cup sun-dried tomatoes
2 tablespoons chopped fresh basil
¼ cup pinenuts
1 cup short grain rice
¾ cup Cabernet Sauvignon wine
2 cups water
½ cup grated Parmesan cheese
Parsley for garnish

Season chops with mustard, salt and pepper. Sauté in the butter until medium rare. Set aside and keep warm.

Add onion, tomatoes, basil, pinenuts and rice. Add wine and water. Simmer, covered, for 20 to 25 minutes, or until rice is cooked. Add cheese to rice, mixing well. Serve rice with lamp chops and garnish with parsley.   Serves 4.

Serve with Cabernet Sauvignon or Pinot Noir.

Lamb Stew Merlot

2 pounds lamp stew meat, carefully trimmed of fat
2 to 3 tablespoons olive oil
1 medium onion, diced
3 medium carrots, diced
2 cloves garlic, minced
2 slices unpeeled orange
1 long strip of lemon peel
1 cup Merlot wine
1 cup tomato juice
1 teaspoon ground cloves
1 stick cinnamon
1 teaspoon powdered coriander
2 tablespoons flour
Salt and pepper

Preheat oven to 325 degrees. In a medium Dutch oven, brown lamb lightly in hot olive oil. Add onions, carrots and garlic; sauté briefly. Add the orange, lemon peel, wine, tomato juice, ground cloves, cinnamon and coriander. Cover and bring to a simmer on top of stove. Place in preheated oven. Bake until tender, about 1 ½ to 2 hours. Check occasionally. If more liquid is needed, add additional equal amounts of wine and tomato juice.

When lamb is tender, remove excess grease, cinnamon stick, orange slices and lemon peel. Thicken sauce with the flour to which you have added a small amount of water to make a paste. Season with salt and pepper. More wine may be added if there is not enough sauce.   Serves 4 to 6.

Serve with a Merlot or Barbera.

Spanish Pork Chops

So very easy to make, it will become a favorite recipe.

4 loin pork chops
⅓ cup uncooked rice
4 medium onions, thinly sliced
2 ½ cups canned, ready-cut tomatoes
Salt and pepper
1 cup Chenin Blanc wine

Place pork chops in buttered casserole or glass baking dish. Put a heaping tablespoon of uncooked rice on each chop. Cover with alternate layers of sliced onions and tomatoes. Season with salt and pepper.

Pour the wine over all. Cover and bake in 350 degree oven for 1 to 1 ½ hours, basting occasionally with juices in the pan. Add more wine if it bakes dry. Leave cover off for the last 15 minutes to brown.   Serves 4.

Serve with Chenin Blanc, Reisling or Zinfandel.

Pork Chops in Ginger-Pear Sauce

A little more work than many recipes, but well worth the extra effort.

2 tablespoons olive oil
4 boneless pork loin chops, ½-inch thick
Dried sage
Salt and pepper
All-purpose flour
2 pears, peeled, cored and thinly sliced
½ cup dry white wine
2 tablespoons sugar
2 tablespoons chopped crystallized ginger

Heat oil in large, heavy skillet over medium heat. Season pork with dried sage, salt and pepper. Coat pork with flour, shake off excess. Put pork in skillet and sauté until brown, about 3 minutes per side. Transfer to a plate.

Drain fat from skillet. Add pears and sauté over medium heat for 2 minutes. Stir in wine, sugar and ginger, scraping up any browned bits. Increase heat to high and boil until pears are tender and syrup is thick, about 5 minutes.

Return pork and juices to skillet. Simmer until cooked through, about 1 minute. Season to taste with salt and pepper. Arrange pork on plates. Spoon sauce over and serve.   Serves 4.

A Chardonnay, Reisling or Gewürztraminer will go well with this.

Baked Ham Steak with Grapes

Combine this recipe with one for risotto to have a definitely different meal.

1 tablespoon butter
2 tablespoons brown sugar
1 center slice boiled ham, 1-inch thick
¾ cup Pinot Noir wine
⅛ teaspoon ground ginger
½ cup seedless white grapes

Melt butter in skillet over low heat; stir in brown sugar. Add the ham. Brown ham on both sides. Transfer to a shallow baking dish. Pour wine over ham; sprinkle with ginger. Bake in 350 degree oven for about 20 minutes.

Transfer ham to hot platter. Pour liquid from baking dish into skillet; add grapes. Heat on top of stove for a few minutes. Pour over ham. Serves 4.

Serve with Pinot Noir or Petit Syrah.

Upside Down Ham Loaf

1 tablespoon butter
½ cup dark brown sugar
1 can (13 ounces) crushed pineapple, drained with
  pineapple juice reserved
6 maraschino cherries, halved
1 egg
½ cup Sherry
1 cup soft bread crumbs
2 tablespoons prepared mustard
1 teaspoon salt
1 ½ pounds ground smoked ham (your butcher can
  grind for you)
½ pound ground fresh pork

Preheat the oven to 350 degrees. Melt the butter in an 8 ×
8 × 2-inch pan. Stir in brown sugar and cover with drained
pineapple and cherries.

Beat egg well, stir in ½ cup of the reserved pineapple juice
and Sherry. Add bread crumbs, mustard, salt, ham and pork.
Mix well and spread over pineapple. Bake for 1 hour. Drain
off excess liquid. Invert on serving platter.   Serves 6 to 8.

Serve with Pinot Noir or Gewürztraminer.

Poultry

Paprika Chicken Ragout

2 broiler-fryer chickens (2 ½ pounds each), cut up
Salt and pepper
⅓ cup butter or margarine
2 medium onions, peeled and chopped
2 tablespoons paprika
2 medium tomatoes, peeled and chopped
1 cup white wine
1 cup chicken broth
2 tablespoons all-purpose flour
2 cups sour cream, at room temperature
3 tablespoons chopped fresh dill

Wipe chicken pieces dry with paper towel. Sprinkle surfaces with salt and pepper. Brown on all sides in heated butter in a skillet. Remove to a plate and keep warm. Add onions to drippings; sauté until tender. Stir in paprika and cook 1 minute. Add tomatoes, wine and chicken broth.

Return chicken pieces to skillet. Cook, covered, about 35 minutes until chicken is tender. Remove chicken and keep warm. Loosen browned bits in bottom of pan, and stir in flour. Gradually add sour cream and cook over low heat, stirring, until thickened and smooth.

To serve, spoon sauce over chicken and sprinkle with dill.
Serves 6 to 8.

Serve with Zinfandel or Reisling.

Chicken Baked in Red Wine

In the Italian countryside, where this dish originated, they prepare this for feast days.

½ teaspoon salt
⅛ teaspoon freshly ground black pepper
2 broiler chickens (1 ¾ to 2 pounds), quartered
1 cup flour
¼ cup peanut oil
1 to 1 ½ cups red wine
1 small yellow onion

Sprinkle salt and pepper generously on both sides of chicken pieces. Put the flour in a paper or plastic bag, and toss two chicken pieces at a time until coated.

In a skillet, lightly brown chicken, using only enough oil to prevent burning. Add more oil as needed. Remove chicken pieces as they brown, adding more until all are browned.

Place chicken, skin side up, in a warm, shallow baking pan. Pour the wine over all. Peel onion and slice into rings on top of chicken.

Bake in a 400 degree oven for about 45 minutes, or until done. Baste occasionally; add more wine if necessary. Remove from oven, baste and serve.   Serves 4.

Serve with Pinot Noir or Merlot.

Don't throw out that bottle of red wine that is turning sour. Just set the bottle aside and in a few weeks, you'll have red wine vinegar.

Chicken Breasts Vermouth

2 teaspoons salt
½ teaspoon allspice
1 teaspoon cinnamon
6 boneless, skinless chicken breasts, cut in half
¼ cup butter
3 scallions, finely chopped
½ cup Dry Vermouth
1 cup heavy cream
½ cup pitted green olives, cut in half lengthwise
¼ cup chopped parsley

Preheat oven to 300 degrees. Place baking dish in oven. Combine salt, allspice and cinnamon; sprinkle mixture on both sides of chicken breasts. Melt butter in a heavy skillet. Sauté the breasts for 5 minutes on each side over low heat. Transfer breasts to hot baking dish. Place in oven. Bake approximately 25 to 30 minutes, or until cooked.

While chicken is cooking, add scallions to butter remaining in skillet. Cook over medium-high heat. When scallions are soft, stir in Vermouth and cream. Stir in accumulated pan juices from chicken; continue to cook until liquid is reduced to less than half. Stir in olives.

Arrange chicken breasts on platter. Pour sauce over breasts. Sprinkle with chopped parsley.   Serves 6 to 8.

Serve with Zinfandel or Gewürztraminer.

Pappardelle with Rock Cornish Hens

1 pound fresh pappardelle pasta
3 tablespoons extra virgin olive oil
6 tablespoons sweet cream butter
1 stalk celery, minced
1 large carrot, minced
4 ounces prosciutto, minced
½ teaspoon fresh sage
2 rock Cornish game hens, cleaned and quartered
1 cup Barbera wine
1 can (18 ounces) Italian plum tomatoes, crushed
1 teaspoon sugar
1 pinch seasoned salt

In a large deep pan, heat the oil and butter. Add the celery, onion, carrot, prosciutto and sage. After about 3 minutes, add the game hens and cook for 5 minutes, stirring. Pour in the wine. When it is nearly evaporated, add the crushed tomatoes, salt, pepper and sugar. Cook over low heat for 45 minutes. If sauce is too thick, add more tomatoes.

When the sauce is almost done, cook the pappardelle (al dente) and drain. Transfer to a large serving bowl or to individual bowls. Top with the sauce and mix well. Then, top with pieces of game hen and serve.   Makes 6 servings.

Suggested wine to accompany this dish is Barbera.

Stuffed Chicken Pinwheels
A very impressive presentation, easily made.

8 whole boneless, skinless chicken breasts
2 bunches scallions, minced
4 cloves garlic, minced or crushed
8 tablespoons butter
16 paper thin slices prosciutto or ham
½ cup chopped Italian parsley
1 tablespoon chopped fresh rosemary (or 1 teaspoon dried)
16 paper thin slices Jack cheese
1 cup Champagne (Brut)

Pound chicken breasts between pieces of plastic wrap until thin. Set aside. Sauté the scallions and garlic in 4 tablespoons of the butter. Cool.

Lay chicken breasts out flat. Place 2 slices of prosciutto or ham on each breast. Spread with the scallion mixture. Sprinkle with the herbs. Top with 2 slices of the cheese. Roll the breasts from the long side, forming a tight roll. Secure with toothpicks or string. Lay the chicken in a foil-lined shallow pan, and dot with the remaining butter. Pour in the Champagne.

Roast in a 350 degree oven for 30 to 40 minutes. Remove the toothpicks or string and slice the chicken rolls into half inch pinwheels. Fan them on serving plates and drizzle with pan juices.   Serves 8.

Serve with Champagne (Brut).

Drunken Chicken
Particularly good when served with rice or bulgur wheat.

1 chicken (2 ½ pounds)
½ cup balsamic vinegar
1 cup Cabernet Sauvignon wine
4 tablespoons olive oil
4 cloves fresh garlic, chopped
½ tablespoon chopped fresh oregano
1 tablespoon chopped fresh basil
1 tablespoon chopped fresh rosemary
1 tablespoon chopped fresh parsley
Salt and pepper

Cut chicken into eight pieces. Mix vinegar, ½ cup of the wine, olive oil, garlic, oregano, basil, rosemary, parsley, salt and pepper. Marinate chicken in mixture overnight.

Remove chicken to baking pan; reserve marinade. Broil until brown, about 15 minutes, turning to brown each side.

Add the reserved marinade and remaining ½ cup wine. Bake at 450 degrees for 45 minutes.   Serves 4 to 6.

Serve with a Cabernet Sauvignon or Chardonnay.

Provencal Chicken Ragout

4 slices bacon, diced
2 to 3 tablespoons olive oil
6 scallions with some tops, minced
1 to 2 cloves garlic, crushed
2 whole chickens, cut up
3 tablespoons all-purpose flour
1 ½ cups dry red wine
1 cup beef bouillon
¼ cup tomato purée
⅓ cup Brandy
1 bay leaf
3 sprigs parsley
½ teaspoon dried thyme
½ teaspoon crumbled dried rosemary
1 teaspoon each salt and pepper
24 small white onions, peeled
24 whole fresh mushrooms, cleaned

Cook bacon in a large skillet to render some of the fat. Add oil, scallions and garlic. Sauté 5 minutes. Wipe chicken pieces dry. Fry, a few at a time, until golden. Set aside.

Spoon off any excess fat. Mix in flour and blend well. Add wine, bouillon, tomato purée, Brandy, bay leaf, parsley, thyme, rosemary, salt and pepper. Mix well and bring to a boil. Add chicken pieces. Lower heat and cook slowly, covered, for 30 minutes. Add onions and continue to cook for 30 minutes longer, until chicken and onions are tender. Add mushrooms during last 10 minutes of cooking. Discard bay leaf and parsley.   Serves 8.

Serve with Pinot Noir, Merlot or Cabernet Sauvignon.

Chicken Rosemary

Very simple, very quick and very, very tasty.

2 tablespoons butter
4 boneless, skinless chicken breasts, lightly floured
½ cup sliced mushrooms
8 canned artichoke hearts, quartered
1 teaspoon chopped fresh rosemary
1 tablespoon lemon juice
½ cup Chardonnay wine
Fresh chopped parsley for garnish
Rosemary sprigs for garnish

Heat butter in a medium sauté pan. Add chicken, mushrooms and artichoke hearts. Sauté 3 to 4 minutes and turn chicken over. Add rosemary and cook until chicken is done. Add lemon juice and wine to sauté pan and reduce until thickened.

Place chicken breasts on warm platter and cover with mushroom and artichoke sauce. Garnish with parsley and a sprig of rosemary.   Serves 4.

Serve with Chardonnay or Sauvignon Blanc.

Chicken Florentine
Florence, Italy, is the source of this recipe that has become a favorite worldwide.

½ pound fresh spinach, stemmed and washed
4 tablespoons butter
1 large onion, cut into rings
1 clove garlic, minced
2 whole boneless, skinless chicken breasts, cut into
  2-inch cubes
½ pound fresh mushrooms, sliced
⅓ cup dry white wine
1 tablespoon flour
1 cup sour cream
1 cup grated sharp cheddar cheese

Steam spinach until wilted. Drain and chop. Melt 2 tablespoons of the butter in a large skillet and sauté onion rings until golden. Remove onions with slotted spoon, mix with spinach and place in buttered casserole.

Add 1 tablespoon of the butter to skillet. Add minced garlic and chicken. Brown chicken and remove to warm plate.

Sauté mushrooms in remaining butter and remove to plate with chicken. Add wine to the pan; then stir in flour. Slowly add sour cream and stir until hot and thickened.

Add chicken, mushrooms and garlic. Place mixture on spinach, sprinkle with cheese and bake uncovered at 350 degrees for 30 to 35 minutes.   Serves 4.

We suggest Chardonnay or Fumé Blanc.

Pan-Roasted Cornish Hens

Yes, lavender as an ingredient. A nice addition to your herbs and spices shelf.

2 Cornish hens, split
3 tablespoons olive oil
½ tablespoon basil
½ teaspoon lavender
½ teaspoon thyme
Salt and black pepper
1 garlic clove, minced
½ cup white wine
1 tablespoon flour

Rub hens with 1 tablespoon of the oil and generously sprinkle herbs on all sides. Season with salt and pepper. Heat the remaining 2 tablespoons of oil in a large, deep skillet over medium-high heat. Add hens.

Brown hens lightly on both sides. Add garlic. Reduce heat to low. Cover and cook 30 to 40 minutes, turning 2 to 3 times, until hens are browned and cooked through.

Remove to warm serving platter; cover to keep warm. Add wine and flour to skillet and cook, stirring to incorporate pan juices and browned bits at the bottom of the skillet until sauce is slightly thickened. Serve hens with pan sauce.

Serves 2 to 4.

Serve a Zinfandel or Chardonnay.

Another gourmet delicacy is created when you thoroughly rub a capon or Cornish hen with Brandy before adding other seasonings.

Chicken in Wine and Olive Sauce

2 tablespoons olive oil
4 large skinless chicken breasts
½ teaspoon salt
¼ teaspoon black pepper
1 large onion, sliced fine
¾ cup white wine
½ cup stuffed green olives, sliced
1 teaspoon chopped fresh thyme
1 teaspoon chopped fresh basil
2 tablespoons all-purpose flour
1 tablespoon water

In a non-stick skillet, heat olive oil over medium-high heat. Add chicken. Sprinkle with ¼ teaspoon of the salt and the pepper. Cook until lightly browned on both sides. Remove to plate.

In same skillet, cook onion in pan drippings until golden, stirring occasionally. Add wine, olives, thyme and basil. Return chicken, with any juices on plate, to the skillet. Reduce heat to low; cover and simmer for 20 to 25 minutes until juices run clear when chicken is pierced. Add more wine if pan becomes too dry during cooking. Remove chicken to warm platter.

In a cup, mix flour, remaining ¼ teaspoon salt and water until smooth. Increase heat to medium high. Pour flour mixture into skillet, whisking constantly. Heat to boiling; boil 1 minute until sauce thickens slightly. Pour sauce over chicken.   Serves 4.

Enjoy with a Gewürztraminer or Zinfandel.

Turkey Sauté with Mustard Cream

We use turkey all the time. This recipe is a good example of its versatility.

2 tablespoons butter
1 tablespoon olive oil
4 skinless turkey fillets (approximately 4 ounces each)
1 medium onion, minced
1 cup dry white wine
⅓ cup chicken broth
⅓ cup half-and-half
2 tablespoons Dijon mustard
Salt and pepper

Heat butter and oil in a large deep frying pan. Add turkey fillets and cook on both sides until light brown. Add the onion and cook for 2 more minutes. Pour the wine and broth over fillets; cover and simmer for 15 to 20 minutes or until tender.

Remove turkey fillets from pan and keep warm. Boil liquid until reduced by half. Remove from heat, stir in the half-and-half and mustard, then heat gently, without boiling. Season to taste. Serve turkey with sauce.   Serves 4.

A Cabernet Sauvignon or Zinfandel will go well with this dish.

Capon Flanders Style

It is said this dish originated during World War I in France with "liberated" chickens and wine.

**1 capon or chicken (6 to 7 pounds), cut in serving
  pieces
3 ½ cups Sauterne or Chenin Blanc wine
1 tablespoon salt
⅛ teaspoon mace
2 tablespoons sugar
6 carrots, cut in julienne strips
3 tablespoons flour
Salt and pepper**

Place capon pieces in a large pot. Add 2 ½ cups of the wine and boiling water to cover. Add salt, mace and sugar. Cover and let come to a boil. Simmer for 2 to 2 ½ hours, or until almost tender.

Add carrots. Cook until carrots are tender. Remove chicken and carrots to hot platter and keep warm. Skim fat from top of stock.

To make the gravy, whisk the flour into 1 cup of the stock until well blended. Stir into remaining stock and add remaining 1 cup of the wine. Cook over medium heat, stirring constantly, until thick and bubbly. Adjust seasoning with salt and pepper. Pour gravy over the chicken and carrots, and serve.   Serves 6.

Serve with Chenin Blanc or Pinot Gris.

Seafood

Seafood

Snapper Poached in Wine with Cucumber and Dill

2 red snapper fillets (7 ounces each)
2 tablespoons peeled, seeded and diced cucumber
½ cup Fumé Blanc wine
¼ cup Crème Fraîche* or heavy cream
2 tablespoons lemon juice
Salt and pepper
1 tablespoon cold butter, cut into pieces
Chopped fresh dill

Place the red snapper in a non-stick pan. Surround with cucumber, add wine. Cover tightly and bring to a bare simmer. Cook until just done, 2 to 3 minutes. Carefully remove the fillets to warm plates.

Rapidly reduce the poaching liquid, then add Crème Fraîche and reduce until the sauce begins to thicken. Add lemon juice and salt and pepper to taste. Add the butter and swirl into mixture. Pour sauce over fish. Sprinkle with dill.
Serves 2.

*Crème Fraîche, a thickened velvety cream, is sold in many supermarkets. A substitute can be made by putting 1 cup of whipping cream and 2 tablespoons buttermilk in a glass container. Stir well, cover and let stand at room temperature for 8 to 12 hours, or until thick.

Serve with Fumé Blanc or Pinot Gris.

Fisherman Stew

All along the coast of the Mediterranean, you'll find this fisherman's stew.

2 tablespoons olive oil
1 large onion, chopped
1 red bell pepper, cored and chopped
1 clove garlic, crushed
4 cups canned, chopped tomatoes, including juice
2 cups red wine
1 cup water
1 tablespoon basil
1 teaspoon thyme
1 teaspoon oregano
¼ teaspoon crushed red pepper
1 teaspoon salt
2 pounds striped sea bass or red snapper fillets,
   skinned and cut into 1-inch cubes

In a large saucepan, heat the oil. Add the onion, red pepper and garlic. Cook until the vegetables are tender. Add the tomatoes, wine, water, basil, thyme, oregano, crushed red pepper and salt. Cover and bring to a boil. Simmer for 10 to 15 minutes.

Add the fish and continue to cook for 5 to 10 minutes more, or until the fish flakes when tested with a fork. Serve with rice or boiled potatoes. Serves 6.

A Pinot Noir or Cabernet Sauvignon will accompany this very well.

Grilled Grouper with Butter Pecan Sauce
It's surprisingly good, this use of honey-roasted pecans with fish.

3 tablespoons finely chopped shallots
¾ cup dry white wine
1 tablespoon wine vinegar
3 tablespoons heavy cream
3 tablespoons chicken stock
3 tablespoons fresh lemon juice
¼ pound butter, chilled
Salt and pepper
⅓ cup honey-roasted pecans
1 ½ pounds grouper fillets, cut in 4 portions
1 tablespoon flour
1 tablespoon olive oil
Fresh chopped parsley for garnish

Combine shallots, wine, vinegar, cream, stock and lemon juice in a medium saucepan and bring to a vigorous boil. Reduce stock down to about ⅓, and lower heat to medium. Whisk in butter, 1 tablespoon at a time, until completely melted. Add salt, pepper and pecans. Set aside.

Prepare fish fillets by lightly dusting them with seasoned flour, brush with olive oil and grill until fish is tender and flaky, 3 to 4 minutes on each side.

To serve, top fish with warm butter pecan sauce and chopped parsley.   Serves 4.

Serve with a Sauvignon Blanc or Reisling.

Seafood St. Jacques

This is the classic Couquilles St. Jacques recipe, to which we have added crab and shrimp.

1 pound scallops
½ cup sliced mushrooms
1 cup Chardonnay or other dry white wine
1 small onion, sliced
1 tablespoon chopped fresh parsley
2 teaspoons lemon juice
1 teaspoon salt
4 tablespoons butter
6 tablespoons flour
1 cup light cream
4 tablespoons shredded Gruyere cheese
¼ pound cooked crabmeat, shredded
½ pound cooked shrimp
Bread crumbs
Paprika

Combine scallops, mushrooms, wine, onion, parsley, lemon juice and salt. Bring to a boil; simmer for 5 minutes. Drain, reserving 1 cup of the liquid.

In a saucepan, melt butter and stir in flour. Add cream and scallop liquid all at once. Stir until mixture thickens, and then add cheese until it melts.

Add scallops, crabmeat and shrimp. Mix well and divide into 6 individual casseroles. Sprinkle with bread crumbs and paprika. Before serving, broil for 1 minute, or until mixture is bubbly.   Serves 6.

Serve with Chardonnay, Chenin Blanc or Reisling.

Southern Seafood Stew

The bayous of Louisiana are the birthplace of this easy-to-make fish stew.

½ pound bacon, diced
2 carrots, finely diced
3 medium onions, thinly sliced
4 cloves garlic, crushed or minced
3 cups fresh or canned plum tomatoes
1 pound small red potatoes, washed and halved
1 cup clam juice
1 cup white wine
½ teaspoon dried thyme
½ teaspoon sugar
2 cups chicken stock
Salt and pepper
¼ teaspoon cayenne pepper
½ pound white fish, cut in small chunks
1 pound medium shrimp, peeled and deveined
2 dozen clams, whole or canned

Sauté the bacon with the carrots, onions and garlic. Drain half the grease. Add the tomatoes, potatoes, clam juice and wine. Sprinkle in the thyme and sugar. Simmer for 30 minutes.

Add the stock. Adjust seasoning with salt, pepper and cayenne pepper. Bring the stew to a low boil. Add the fish, shrimp and clams. Simmer briefly until the fish is just cooked. Serve hot with crusty French bread.   Serves 8.

Serve with Chardonnay, Fumé Blanc or Reisling.

Scallops Wrapped in Smoked Salmon with Pasta
Looking for something elegant and different? This is it.

20 large scallops
20 pieces of thinly sliced smoked salmon
Salt and pepper
2 tablespoons fresh thyme
¼ cup Chardonnay wine
6 tablespoons butter
14 ounces angel hair pasta
2 tablespoons vegetable stock or ⅓ cup wine
1 fresh tomato, cubed
Radicchio and thyme for garnish

Wrap scallops in smoked salmon and put in baking pan. Sprinkle with salt, pepper, fresh thyme and wine. Brush with 2 tablespoons of the butter and bake for 5 minutes in a preheated 450 degree oven.

Boil pasta for 3 to 5 minutes. Remove pasta and put in a frying pan with vegetable stock, salt and pepper. Simmer and thicken with the remaining butter.

To serve, place some pasta on a plate. Arrange 5 pieces of wrapped scallop on top. Garnish with tomato cubes, radicchio and thyme.   Serves 4.

Serve with Chardonnay or Chenin Blanc.

Halibut Almond

2 pounds halibut steak
2 tablespoons butter
2 tablespoons minced onion
⅔ cup white wine
Salt, pepper and paprika
⅓ cup toasted slivered almonds
Parsley for garnish

Place halibut in a shallow baking dish; dot with butter. Sprinkle with onions. Pour wine over all. Sprinkle with salt, pepper and paprika. Cover tightly with foil and bake in a 375 degree oven for 20 minutes or until fish flakes at the touch of a fork.

To serve, sprinkle with almonds and garnish with parsley.
Serves 4 to 6.

Serve with Fumé Blanc or Chardonnay.

Louisiana Fish Ragout

From France to Nova Scotia to New Orleans, this recipe is now a classic.

1 large onion, peeled and chopped
2 cloves garlic, crushed
1 medium green bell pepper, cleaned and chopped
3 tablespoons olive oil
1 can (16 ounces) tomatoes, chopped
1 bay leaf
1 tablespoon Worcestershire sauce
1 teaspoon dried basil
⅛ teaspoon cayenne pepper
1 teaspoon salt
½ teaspoon pepper
1 cup uncooked long grain rice
1 cup white wine
1 cup chicken broth
1 pound red snapper, cut in large cubes
3 tablespoons chopped fresh parsley

Sauté onion, garlic and green bell pepper in heated oil in a large kettle for 5 minutes. Add tomatoes, bay leaf, Worcestershire sauce, basil, cayenne, salt and pepper. Cook slowly, uncovered, for 5 minutes.

Add rice, wine and chicken broth. Cook slowly, covered, for 25 minutes. Add fish cubes and cook about 15 minutes longer, until rice and fish are tender. Mix in parsley. Remove bay leaf before serving.   Serves 4 to 6.

Serve with Pinot Gris or Sauvignon Blanc.

Salmon with Fresh Herbs in a Cream Sauce

A very rich, creamy wine sauce that complements the salmon perfectly.

½ cup dry white wine
1 cup whipping cream
4 tablespoons butter, at room temperature
4 skinless salmon fillets (6 to 8 ounces each)
½ cup Dry Vermouth
1 large shallot, minced
2 tablespoons minced assorted fresh herbs (tarragon,
  basil, dill and chives)
2 tablespoons fresh lemon juice
Salt and pepper

Preheat oven to 400 degrees. Boil wine in a heavy small saucepan until reduced to 2 tablespoons, about 5 minutes. Add cream and boil until reduced to ½ cup, about 10 minutes. Set aside.

Use ½ tablespoon of the butter to grease a large oven-proof skillet. Arrange salmon in single layer in skillet. Pour Vermouth over. Top with shallot. Bring to simmer. Cover skillet with foil and place in oven. Bake salmon until just cooked through, about 10 minutes.

Transfer salmon to a platter. Tent with foil. Mix liquid in skillet into sauce. Cook over medium heat until reduced to a sauce consistency, stirring occasionally. Remove from heat. Whisk in the remaining butter and then the minced herbs. Season sauce with lemon juice, salt and pepper. Spoon over salmon.   Serves 4.

Serve with a Chardonnay.

Seafood Casserole

The French coast of the Mediterranean is the source of this recipe.

¼ cup extra virgin olive oil
1 ½ cups minced onions
1 cup julienned red bell pepper
1 ½ cups peeled and diced potatoes
½ teaspoon pepper
½ clove garlic, minced
2 bay leaves
2 cups Chardonnay wine
4 teaspoons tomato paste
1 pound fillet of sole, cut into bite-sized pieces
1 pound raw shrimp, shelled and deveined, cut in half
½ pound cooked crabmeat, shredded
2 teaspoons minced parsley

Heat oil in a casserole and sauté onions over low heat for 10 minutes. Add red bell pepper and potatoes and cook for 5 minutes. Add pepper, garlic, bay leaves, wine and tomato paste. Cover and cook over low heat for 20 minutes.

Add sole; cook for 5 minutes. Mix in shrimp and cook, covered, for an additional 7 minutes or until shrimp turn pink. Do not overcook the fish. Add crabmeat and cook just to heat through. Remove bay leaves. Sprinkle with parsley.
Serves 6 to 8.

Serve with Chardonnay or Fumé Blanc.

Seafood

Baked Lobster

2 ounces butter
2 cups sliced mushrooms
1 cup diced green bell peppers
1 ½ cups Sherry
1 dash of salt
1 dash of black pepper
4 cups white sauce
½ cup diced pimientos
4 whole lobsters (3 pounds each), boiled and cooked
4 teaspoons grated Parmesan cheese

To make the basic sauce, melt butter in a large saucepan. Add the mushrooms and green bell peppers. Cook until tender. Add paprika and stir in Sherry. Cook until liquid is reduced by half. Add salt and pepper, then white sauce and pimientos. Blend well; bring to a simmer.

The lobster can be prepared while vegetables are cooking. Remove claws and knuckles from lobster. Hold lobster with its top side up. With kitchen shears, cut an oval opening in top of shell from tip of tail to base of head. Remove meat from body, claws and knuckles. Cut into large dice. Discard intestinal vein and stomach (a hard sac near the head) before dicing.

Add meat to sauce and simmer for 10 minutes. Divide mixture evenly and spoon back into lobster shell. Dust with Parmesan cheese and brown in a 375 degree oven for 15 minutes.   Serves 4.

Serve with a dry Chenin Blanc or Reisling.

Desserts

Pumpkin Walnut Cake with Chocolate Wine Sauce

1 ½ cups walnuts, coarsely chopped
1 ½ cups bittersweet chocolate chips
3 cups flour
3 teaspoons baking powder
1 teaspoon ground cinnamon
1 teaspoon ground ginger
½ teaspoon freshly grated nutmeg
1 cup sweet butter, softened
2 cups sugar
1 ½ cups pumpkin purée
4 eggs
¾ cup Champagne (Brut)
8 ounces semi-sweet baking chocolate, chopped
¾ cup Port

Toss the nuts and chocolate chips in ½ cup of the flour. Set aside. Sift the remaining dry ingredients, except sugar. Set aside. Cream the butter and sugar in a mixing bowl until fluffy. Beat in the pumpkin and then the eggs, one at a time.

Fold in the dry ingredients, alternately with the Champagne. Fold in the nuts and chocolate. Pour into a greased and floured 10-inch tube or bundt pan. Bake 1 hour and 15 minutes at 325 degrees. Cool and remove from the pan.

To prepare Chocolate Wine Sauce, melt semi-sweet chocolate and Port in a double boiler over hot water, whisking until smooth. Serve cake in slices, topped with whipped cream and Chocolate Wine Sauce. Serves 12.

Serve with Champagne (Brut).

Chocolate Zucchini Loaf Cake
No, you can't taste the zucchini. It's there to make the cake light and moist.

1 cup unsweetened powdered cocoa
1 cup sugar
2 tablespoons poppy seeds
2 cups flour
1 teaspoon baking powder
1 teaspoon baking soda
½ teaspoon salt
1 teaspoon cinnamon
½ teaspoon nutmeg
½ cup vegetable oil
2 eggs, beaten
½ cup milk
¼ cup Zinfandel wine
1 cup shredded zucchini

Mix all dry ingredients together. Blend in oil and eggs. Add milk; mix well. Add wine and stir. Fold in zucchini. Stir all ingredients together well.

Pour into a greased 5 × 8-inch loaf pan. Bake in a 325 degree oven for 60 to 70 minutes.   Serves 6 to 8.

Serve with a Late Harvest Zinfandel or Muscat Canelli.

Brandied Fruit Cake

Be sure to use Brandy which is at least five years old.

1 ½ cups dark raisins
1 cup golden raisins
2 ½ cups chopped dried figs
1 cup Brandy
1 ½ cups butter
2 ½ cups brown sugar
1 tablespoon cinnamon
½ tablespoon allspice
½ tablespoon nutmeg
½ tablespoon cloves
5 eggs
1 ¼ cups raspberry jam
5 cups unbleached white flour, sifted together with 1
  tablespoon baking soda
2 ½ cups toasted and chopped walnuts or pecans

Soak the raisins and figs in the Brandy for at least 2 hours.

In a large bowl, cream butter, then add brown sugar and spices. Cream until light. Add eggs separately, beating after each addition. Stir in jam. Add flour and baking soda gradually, stirring to combine mixture.

Fold in toasted chopped nuts and soaked raisins and figs. Pour into prepared (buttered and floured) loaf pans. Bake in a preheated 325 degree oven for 40 minutes to 1 hour. While still warm, brush each cake liberally with Brandy.

When cool, wrap in plastic wrap and keep in a tightly closed tin.   Makes 4 large loaves.

Serve with Tawny Port or Cream Sherry.

Brandied Rice Pudding

Takes rice pudding to an entirely new plateau in desserts.

½ cup raisins
½ cup Brandy
3 cups cooked rice
2 sliced apples
Grated rind and juice of ½ orange
Grated rind and juice of ½ lemon
2 egg yolks, beaten
½ cup sugar
1 teaspoon ground cinnamon
2 egg whites, beaten to soft peak

Soak raisins in Brandy for at least an hour to soften. Mix all ingredients except egg whites together. Fold in egg whites last.

Bake in greased 8-inch round casserole in a 350 degree oven for 1 hour. Serve warm with whipped cream, if desired.
Serves 6.

Serve with Brandy or Champagne (Brut).

Smooth-skinned lemons have lots more juice than rough-skinned lemons, but rough-skinned lemons grate better. To get more juice, heat a lemon in boiling water for about 3 minutes, or place in a microwave for 1 minute on low.

Port Fruit Cake

There is nothing better to have handy for holiday entertaining.

1 ½ cups chopped mixed dried fruit
1 cup Port
1 cup sugar
2 cups flour
1 teaspoon ground cloves
2 teaspoons baking powder
1 teaspoon baking soda
½ cup margarine, softened, not melted
1 egg beaten
Grated rind of one orange
¼ cup orange juice
½ cup chopped walnuts

The day or night before baking, soak chopped dried fruit in the Port.

Mix together sugar, flour, cloves, baking powder and baking soda. Add softened margarine and blend with fork to make fine crumbs. Next, blend to moisten, but do not over-mix, beaten egg, grated orange rind, orange juice, chopped walnuts, chopped fruit and remaining Port liquid.

Pour in a 5 × 9-inch loaf pan. Bake at 350 degrees for one hour.   Serves 8 to 10.

Serve with a Tawny Port.

Chocolate Bread Pudding
*For 3 generations, this recipe has been in our family.
Our generation added the Brandy!*

2 eggs
1 ½ cups fine, soft bread crumbs
3 cups milk, scalded
1 tablespoon butter
⅔ cup sugar
1 teaspoon cinnamon
¼ teaspoon salt
3 squares unsweetened chocolate, melted
1 teaspoon vanilla
2 tablespoons Brandy
½ cup semi-sweet chocolate chips

Beat eggs, then add bread crumbs, milk, butter, sugar, cinnamon and salt. Mix well. Add melted chocolate, vanilla and Brandy. Fold in chocolate chips. Pour into a greased baking dish and bake in a preheated 325 degree oven until firm. Serve hot or cold with whipped cream.   Serves 8.

Serve with Champagne or Tawny Port.

Apple Cake

A nice, moist, light cake which is just right to finish a big meal, or to eat as a snack.

1 cup golden raisins
½ cup Zinfandel wine
2 ¾ cups flour
1 ½ teaspoons baking soda
1 ½ teaspoons cinnamon
½ teaspoon baking powder
½ teaspoon salt
½ teaspoon nutmeg
¼ teaspoon allspice
¼ teaspoon ginger
¾ cup butter, at room temperature
1 ¾ cups sugar
3 large or 4 medium eggs, beaten
1 ¾ cups unsweetened applesauce

Soak raisins in gently boiling wine for 10 minutes. Mix all dry ingredients. Blend butter and sugar together. Add eggs and flour mixture to butter mixture, alternating eggs and flour little by little.

Fold in raisins and applesauce. Pour into buttered and floured bundt pan. Bake at 350 degrees for 1 hour or until done.   Serves 8 to 10.

Recommended wine: A Riesling or a Zinfandel.

Brandied Apple Cranberry Pie

Crunchy, colorful and flavorful. Make one, and you'll agree it is a great apple pie.

4 cups peeled and cubed apples
1 cup fresh cranberries
¾ cup chopped toasted walnuts
Zest and juice of 1 lemon
1 cup sugar
1 teaspoon cinnamon
¼ cup flour
½ cup Brandy
1 unbaked 9-inch prepared pie shell
2 tablespoons butter
Sugar and cinnamon

Mix apples, cranberries and walnuts. Sprinkle with lemon juice. Add lemon zest and stir in the sugar, cinnamon and flour. Mix well. Add Brandy and let marinate for 15 minutes.

Pour into pie shell, dot with butter, and cover with vented upper crust. Crimp edges and sprinkle with additional cinnamon and sugar.

Bake for 10 minutes in a preheated 450 degree oven, then lower temperature to 350 degrees and bake for another 30 to 45 minutes, until crust is brown and apples are cooked.

Serve while still warm. Accompany with cheese. Serves 6.

Serve with Brandy or Tawny Port.

Fresh Pears Poached in Wine with Chocolate Sauce

A very elegant dessert that you can make a few days ahead and serve in minutes.

6 large, firm fresh pears
5 cups white wine
1 cup sugar
6 cloves
2 cinnamon sticks
1 cup heavy cream
4 squares bitter chocolate
2 ½ cups powdered sugar
½ cup butter
½ cup strong coffee
1 pint vanilla ice cream

Peel pears, leaving the stems. Core from the bottom. Bring the wine, sugar, cloves and cinnamon to a boil in a saucepan. Place the pears in the wine and simmer until tender; do not overcook. Set aside and let pears cool in the wine.

Make chocolate sauce by putting cream, chocolate, powdered sugar, butter and coffee in a double boiler. Heat for 30 minutes or until the chocolate is melted. Mix well.

To serve, drain the pears, spoon the chocolate sauce on individual plates and place a pear in the center with a scoop of vanilla ice cream at its side. Drizzle a little more chocolate sauce over the pear and garnish with fresh mint. Serves 6.

Serve with a Zinfandel or Champagne.

Custard with Strawberries in Muscat Canelli
You bring the Italian countryside into your home with this traditional dessert.

2 cups milk
Slivered zest of 2 oranges
2 eggs
4 egg yolks
½ cup sugar
1 teaspoon vanilla
1 ⅔ cups Muscat Canelli wine
2 cups halved strawberries

Scald milk with the orange zest. In large mixing bowl, beat the eggs and lightly stir in the sugar. Add the milk slowly, stirring constantly. Add the vanilla and blend well. Strain to remove zest and pour into 6 custard cups.

Place the cups in a shallow baking pan. Fill the pan with boiling water to ½ way up the sides of the cups. Bake in center of a preheated 350 degree oven for about 35 minutes until the custard feels firm when pressed. Remove from water, cool and then chill in refrigerator for at least 2 hours.

Meanwhile, put wine in small saucepan. Bring to a boil and reduce to ¼ cup, or syrup consistency; chill. Toss with strawberries 30 minutes before serving. Unmold custard onto individual plates. Surround with strawberries; drizzle with the syrup that remains from the strawberries. Serve immediately.   Serves 6.

You'll enjoy Muscat Canelli with this dessert.

Brandied Chocolate Pecan Pie

One 9-inch packaged pie crust
FILLING:
1 cup light corn syrup
½ cup sugar
¼ cup margarine or butter, melted
1 teaspoon vanilla
3 tablespoons Brandy
1 teaspoon cinnamon
3 eggs
1 cup semi-sweet chocolate chips
1 ½ cups pecan halves
TOPPING:
1 pint whipped cream
½ teaspoon cinnamon
1 teaspoon powdered sugar
1 tablespoon Brandy

Unfold pie crust and make according to package directions, using a 9-inch pie pan. Heat oven to 325 degrees.

In a large bowl, combine corn syrup, sugar, margarine, vanilla, Brandy, cinnamon and eggs and beat well. Stir in chocolate chips and pecans. Spread evenly in pie crust-lined pan. Bake at 325 degrees for 55 to 65 minutes or until deep golden brown and filling is set. Cover edge of pie crust with strip of foil after 15 to 20 minutes of baking to prevent excessive browning. Cool completely.

Garnish pie with whipped cream to which you have added cinnamon, powdered sugar and Brandy.   Serves 8.

Serve with Muscat Canelli or Pink Champagne.

Nut Wine Cake

This is an old English recipe that we have updated.

½ cup butter
2 cups sugar
6 egg yolks, beaten
2 cups sifted flour
½ teaspoon baking powder
¼ teaspoon salt
1 teaspoon powdered cocoa
½ teaspoon cinnamon
1 cup milk
¼ cup Port
1 cup finely chopped Brazil nuts
3 egg whites, beaten

In a large bowl, beat butter and sugar until creamy. Add egg yolks and beat well. Sift flour, baking powder, salt, cocoa and cinnamon together. Add to the mixture alternately with milk and wine. Stir in chopped nuts. Gently fold in beaten egg whites.

Pour batter into greased and floured 10-inch baking pan. Bake for 1 hour in a 375 degree oven. Serve warm.

Serves 6 to 8.

Serve with Port or Cream Sherry.

Chocolate Brownies with Port Cream

4 squares (4 ounces) unsweetened baking chocolate,
  chopped into bits
4 squares (4 ounces) semi-sweet baking chocolate,
  chopped into bits
8 ounces (2 cubes) butter
1 ¾ cups granulated sugar
7 eggs
1 tablespoon vanilla
1 teaspoon salt
1 cup flour
½ cup chopped walnuts
1 cup Port
1 cup whipping cream
¼ cup sugar
1 teaspoon vanilla

Generously butter an 8 ×13-inch baking pan. Heat chocolate
with butter in a double boiler until completely melted.
Remove from the heat and stir in sugar to partially dissolve.
Beat the eggs; add vanilla. In a separate bowl, sift the flour
and salt together. Stir the egg into melted chocolate, and
then stir in the flour and walnuts just until combined; don't
over-stir. Spread into buttered pan and bake in a preheated
350 degree oven for 30 minutes.

To prepare Port Cream, simmer Port over medium-high heat
until reduced to ¼ cup. Chill. Beat cream until it begins to
thicken, then stream in the sugar, Port and vanilla. Continue
to beat to soft peak. Cool brownies completely before
cutting. Serve with a dollop of Port Cream. Serves 8 to 10.

Enjoy with a Tawny Port or Champagne.

Brandied Bananas
Very elegant, yet very easy and fast to make.

3 ripe but firm bananas
½ cup orange juice
½ cup Brandy
¼ cup brown sugar
½ teaspoon cinnamon
¼ cup grated coconut
3 tablespoons butter or margarine
½ cup whipping cream

Peel bananas, slice lengthwise, and arrange cut-side down in glass baking plate. Cover with sauce of orange juice mixed with the Brandy.

Sprinkle with brown sugar, cinnamon, and grated coconut. Dot with butter. Bake in a 350 degree oven for 20 minutes. Serve with whipped cream.   Serves 6.

Serve with Brandy or Champagne (Brut).

Baked bananas? Peel bananas, then place them in a baking dish, brush with lime juice, and a little white wine mixed with honey. Dot with butter and bake at 400 degrees for 25 to 30 minutes. Or to microwave, place in a dish, then cover with plastic wrap which has been pierced 2 to 3 times. Microwave at the power and time suggested.

Poached Fresh Pears in Champagne with Chocolate Sauce

These pears are excellent served over French vanilla ice cream and topped with chocolate sauce.

6 large fresh pears
1 ½ quarts Champagne (Brut)
1 cup sugar
6 cloves
2 cinnamon sticks
1 cup heavy cream
4 squares bitter chocolate
2 ½ cups powdered sugar
½ cup butter
½ cup strong coffee

Select large firm pears. Peel pears, leaving the stems. Core from the bottom, leaving a ¾-inch hole. Bring the Champagne, sugar and seasonings to a boil in a saucepan. Place the pears in the wine and simmer until tender. Be careful not to overcook. Set aside and let the pears cool in the wine.

In a double boiler, heat the cream, chocolate, powdered sugar, butter and coffee for 30 minutes, or until the chocolate is melted. Mix well.

Drain the pears, spoon the chocolate sauce in a nice stem glass or a bowl, and place the pears in the center. Garnish with fresh mint leaves.   Serves 6.

Serve with Champagne (Brut).

Tiramisu
The classic Italian dessert.

5 tablespoons sugar
2 egg yolks
2 ounces softened cream cheese
5 ⅜ ounces Mascarpone cheese
3 teaspoons plus 1 ounce Marsala wine
7 ounces heavy whipping cream, whipped
2 cups espresso or strong coffee
½ cup warm water
24 ladyfinger cookies
3 tablespoons powdered sweetened cocoa mix

In an electric mixer, prepare cream mixture by whipping 3 tablespoons of the sugar and egg yolks on high speed until pale yellow and thick. With mixer on medium speed, add cream cheese and whip until smooth. Add Mascarpone and 3 teaspoons of the Marsala. Mix until incorporated. Fold in whipped cream. Refrigerate.

Combine espresso, remaining 1 ounce Marsala, remaining 2 tablespoons sugar and the warm water.

To assemble, dip ladyfingers in espresso mixture. Place one layer of dipped ladyfingers on the bottom of a serving platter. Top with one layer of cream mixture. Add another layer of dipped ladyfingers, topped with a second layer of cream mixture. Sift cocoa over top.   Serves 4.

Suggested wine to accompany this dish: Moscato Canelli.

Cooking with Wine

You can pair wine with food as an ingredient and as an accompaniment. Because wine has been used in cooking for centuries, certain guidelines have been developed to help choose which wines go best with certain foods.

If you are cooking with a hearty red wine, serve a hearty red wine to go with your meal. It does not have to be the same varietal, but should be the same type. For example, if you used a Cabernet Sauvignon for roasting beef, serve Cabernet Sauvignon, Pinot Noir, or Barbera with the meal. The same is true of white wines. If you poach salmon with a dry Chardonnay, serve a Chardonnay, Chenin Blanc or Sauvignon Blanc.

Generally, serving red wine to accompany dishes which have been cooked with white wine just doesn't taste very good. The same is true of serving a white wine with a dish cooked with red wine.

If you want wine before the meal, we suggest Champagne or Sparkling Wine as the easiest choice because they go well with nuts (excluding peanuts), cheeses, pâtés, quiches, crudities, etc. Other choices would include Reisling, Chardonnay, White Zinfandel or Chenin Blanc.

The recipes in this cookbook all have wines selected by the chef who created the recipe. Here are some suggestions for wine to add to your own favorite recipes:

Cooking with Wine

Measurements are per pound, unless otherwise noted.

<u>Soups</u> (Add just prior to serving.)
For clear and cream soups . Dry Sherry, 1 tsp per portion
For meat soups . . . . Red or White, 1 tsp per portion
For vegetable soups . . . . Red or White, 1 tsp per portion

<u>Meats</u> *(Add after browning, or as a marinade, or both.)*
For Beef . . . . Red or Brandy, ¼ cup
For Lamb . . . . White, ¼ cup
For Veal . . . . White, ¼ cup
For Ham . . . . White or Port, 2 cups (basting)

<u>Pastas</u>
With tomato sauce . . . . Red, ¼ cup per portion
With cream sauce . . . . White, ¼ cup per portion

<u>Poultry</u>
For roasted Chicken . . . . White, ½ cup (basting)
For poached Chicken . . . . White, ½ cup
For roasted Turkey . . . . . . White or Red, ¼ cup (basting)
For Cornish Hens . . . . White or Red, ¼ cup (basting)
For Duck . . . . Red or Brandy, ¼ cup (basting)
For Goose . . . . Red or Brandy, ¼ cup (basting)

<u>Seafood</u> *(Add prior to cooking.)*
For poached Freshwater Fish . . . . White, ¼ cup
For fine-textured Saltwater Fish . . . . White, ¼ cup
For coarse-textured Saltwater Fish . . . . Red, ¼ cup
For sautéed Fish . . . . White, 4 tablespoons
For Shellfish . . . . White, ¼ cup

Deciphering The Restaurant Wine List

Most restaurants have their wine lists organized by type: Red Wines, White Wines and Champagnes or Sparkling Wines. They may have a wine list of twenty or more wines by the bottle, and a few by the glass. Most of these lists start with the highest priced wines in each category and work their way down to the least expensive.

When the wines are listed by name, winery, vintage, estate, etc., you have some guideline as to why one wine may cost four or five times more than another wine.

But when you have only the name of the winery, type of wine, and price, it can be quite a bit more difficult.

If the wine list is presented by the restaurant's sommelier (wine specialist) you can get expert guidance as to what wine to order with your meal. Don't hesitate to tell him/her what you are going to eat, and tell him what price range you want to order from. A sommelier has been trained in wines and has passed examinations to become qualified. He should be able to tell you about the differences and will recommend a wine to pair with your food choice.

Most servers in good restaurants are trained to help you select appropriate wines for the specialty dishes of the restaurant.

But, in any case, if you are told that the most expensive wines on the list are the ideal choice, you are being conned into spending more money than is necessary.

Deciphering the Wine List

In those cases where the server simply isn't qualified, you can be reasonably sure of getting a good bottle of wine with two simple rules: Order an American wine; and select a wine that is about a third of the way down on the list.

Selecting wines sold by the glass presents less of a problem since your choice is more limited. Usually a restaurant will have three or four whites, a blush and a few reds. Some will have Champagne, but that will usually be a split (half bottle).

Wine by the glass may have the winery and the name of the wine identified on the wine list. Since all will be at the same or similar price, the quality will be pretty equal.

Some restaurants are now offering a higher-priced line of wines by the glass labeled as "Reserve Wines". Here too, the quality will be about equal in this category. The author has not found great differences between the quality of the regular menu of wines by the glass and "Reserve Wines", but that is a matter of taste.

If the wine is labeled "House Wine" and not identified, ask the server whose it is. If you are told that he doesn't know because it is bottled for the restaurant, avoid it. Go without rather than order it. There are a few very rare exceptions to this rule, but they are very few and very, very rare.

One more thing. If the wine, whether by bottle or glass is "off" or tastes sour or rancid, or is simply bad, don't hesitate to reject it. That's why the server has the person who orders the wine taste a sip first. The wine may have been stored improperly or it may have been a bad lot. Don't assume it is good until you taste it.

The restaurant has priced its wines to absorb this loss. (Average price of a bottle of wine in a restaurant, as compared to a wine merchant, is 200% to 300% more.) So, if it isn't good, refuse it. It's your money, isn't it?

Serving Wine

You have been told for years that
red wines should be served at
room temperature, which can vary
more than twenty degrees. We
suggest that you will like it cool,
but not cold, and certainly not hot.
If you place it in the refrigerator
two hours before serving, remove
it one hour before and open the
bottle to let the wine breathe, you
will have a desirable temperature
for your red wine.

White wines, and particularly Champagne, require chilling.
Place them in the refrigerator for two hours before serving.
If it's warm in the room, place the bottle half submerged in
a bucket of ice to keep it well chilled.

There are at least two thousand different types of bottle
openers. Of them, there are 2 that are the easiest to use.
One is the screw type, with two wings that remove the cork
simply by pushing the wings down when the screw is
embedded in the cork. The other is the waiter's screw type,
which also has a knife to cut the foil around the cork. Each
costs less than five dollars.

Champagne corks are easy to remove if you simply unwire
them, put a cloth over the cork and twist the bottle gently –
not the cork – and ease the cork out of the bottle.

Serving Wine

Quite honestly, you can serve wine in a jelly glass and it will taste good. It will, however, taste better if served in the proper glass. Here are the 4 glasses that you really should have to enjoy your wine to its utmost: the Champagne flute, the Balloon glass, the Brandy snifter, and the Sherry glass. Each glass can cost as little as a few dollars, or you can go for crystal and spend as much as you like.

Enjoy!

BALLOON WINE
8-14 Ounces

CHAMPAGNE FLUTE
6-8 Ounces

SHERRY
2-4 Ounces

BRANDY SNIFTER
6-12 Ounces

American
Wines

A Simple Guide To American Wines

There are four categories of wines: *Appetizer* or *Aperitif Wines, Sparkling Wines, Still or Table Wines,* and *Dessert or Fortified Wines.* All wines are in one of two types: Sparkling Wines and Still Wines. The Sparkling Wines have bubbles; the Still Wines do not.

Appetizer or Aperitif Wines: These wines are customarily served before a meal, and often have flavors added to them. The best examples of these are Sherry and Port. Both have more than 14% alcohol content, the legal limit for a wine in America. (The U.S. Government says that if it is more than 14%, it is liquor and is taxed accordingly.)

Sparkling Wines: There are two kinds of Sparkling Wines produced in this country: Champagne and Sparkling Wine. Champagne is made by the Champenoise method, which is the traditional European process of aging the wine in the bottle. Sparkling Wines are made by the Charmat method which ages the wine in large tanks before bottling.

In America, unlike Europe where the governments strictly control the use of the word "Champagne", many wines aged in the bottle that might be called Champagne are labeled Sparkling Wine, and some wines aged in tanks are called Champagne. These American Champagnes and Sparkling Wines are available in the traditional blanc (white) and in rosé (pink). All have varying degrees of sweetness, and have one of the following labels:

Natural or Extra Brut is the driest, with no hint of sweetness.
Brut is dry, with little or no sweetness.

Extra-Dry is a little sweet.
Sec is sweet.
Demi-Sec is very sweet.

Still and Table Wines: These wines are divided into Varietals, Proprietaries, Appellations and Generics.

Varietals are wines that have been given the name of the grapes from which they were made. Each wine must contain at least 75% of the specific variety to earn the right to use the name of the grape. The remaining percentage may be made up of grape varieties that the winemaker uses to achieve flavor, provide color or control cost. Some examples of Varietals are Chardonnay, Gewürztraminer and Merlot. Usually quite inexpensive, these wines are a safe and easy choice for the novice wine buyer.

Proprietaries are wines that the winemaker produces labeled under a brand name. These are usually the result of blending several varieties of lower cost grapes to produce a unique body, flavor, and aroma that can be found only in that particular wine. Examples of these are "Turning Leaf", "Blue Nun", "Soleo", and "Tessera". Most of these wines are moderately priced.

Appellation in the labeling of wines is relatively new in America. In France, "Champagne" took its name from the Champagne region. "Rhine" comes from the Rhine River in Germany. The name of the wine comes from the region in which the grapes are grown, not where the wine was made.

In 1982, the U.S. Government established "American Viticultural Areas" which specified the areas of unique grape growing regions, and the names for wines of that region.

These regions can be large, such as the entire Ohio Valley grape-growing region, smaller, such as the Willamette Valley in Oregon, or just a few square miles such as the Stag's Leap district in California.

The use of an Appellation requires that 85% of the grapes in the wine must come from that region. An additional element in this category is the right to specify the vineyard's name as part of the appellation if there is a minimum of 95% of the winery's own grapes, grown in that region, in the wine produced. These are customarily labeled "Estate Bottled".

Wines that are designated by region in addition to the variety of grape used in its making are usually the better American wines. When it also carries the vineyard name where the grapes were grown, it is often a superior wine.

Generic wines are like generic drugs and foods. They are simply called "Red Wine", "White Wine", or "Blush Wine". "Jug" wines in large bottles or boxes are usually generic.

The winemaker may use a single variety of grapes or a blend of varieties which may come from different regions or even different countries. There can be great differences in the quality of the wine you purchase from one bottle to another, particularly from different harvest seasons. These are wines that should be tasted before being served.

Vintage, the year the grapes were harvested, is often used to specify a particularly fine harvest with grapes that were above-average quality, and thus produced a superior wine.

The vintage year is very important in European wines due to the drastic changes in the weather in the grape-growing regions. In America, the weather in most grape-growing regions is not that variable, therefore most years are considered vintage years.

Dessert or Fortified Wines: These are classified as being wines that have more than 14% alcohol, and are generally served with dessert. Port, Sherry and Sauterne lead the list in popularity.

The Most Popular American Wines

Listed here are the most popular varietal wines made in the United States. There are many other wines, some of them unique to a particular region of the country. This listing will give you the basic information about the leading ones.

Red Wines

Cabernet Sauvignon is a classic wine with a rich, intense flavor with undertones of raspberry and cassis. Best if aged a few years.

Merlot is similar to Cabernet Sauvignon, but with a mellower and softer taste. Relatively new in America, it has become very popular due to its versatility in pairing with many different foods.

Pinot Noir is a spicy rich wine that, like Merlot, is growing in popularity because it goes so well with many different foods.

Zinfandel is vinted in a wide variety of wines ranging from a dark, fruity full-bodied wine, to a light Blush in a White Zinfandel. A Late Harvest Zinfandel, with increased sugars, is growing in popularity as a dessert or sweet wine.

Cabernet Franc, originally brought to the U.S. for blending, is now bottled under its own name. It is quite similar to Cabernet Sauvignon.

Petit Syrah is a big, full-bodied wine, with peppery overtones. It is also often used to blend with other red wines to add body and character.

Barbera is a dark red wine with a rich, fruity flavor. Relatively new in the U.S., it is rapidly overtaking the long time Italian import, Chianti.

Gamay is a very light, fragrant wine and is particularly popular when accompanying light summer meals.

Carigniane is a heavy-bodied rich table wine, particularly well suited to accompany hearty beef dishes, such as stews.

Grenache is pale in color, but has good fruity overtones. It is a nice change from the more full bodied red wines.

White Wines

Champagne (Sparkling Wine) is the most popular of all white wines. Available in various degrees of dryness and in a Blush, it is a year-round favorite. Its popularity can be attributed to the fact that it is an excellent beverage, and also goes well with so many foods.

Chardonnay comes close to Champagne in popularity with its wide range of tastes from a rich, buttery wine to a very dry wine. The most versatile of all white wines, it goes well with nearly any food.

Sauvignon Blanc, also marketed under the name Fumé Blanc, is a wine with undertones of herbs. Quite dry, it accompanies many foods extremely well.

Reisling, also known as Johannisberg Reisling, is known for its wonderful range of flavors, ranging from very dry to sweet. A classic in Europe for centuries, it is now being grown and vinted in California and Washington and is becoming increasingly popular in the Eastern states. It is very compatible with light foods, such as chicken, fish and salads.

Most Popular American Wines

Gewürztraminer's crisp, spicy characteristics, coupled with its clear and pungent flavor have made it a very popular wine in America. Produced in many degrees of sweetness ranging from very dry to very sweet, it is a pleasant light wine. Late Harvest Gewürztraminer is a very sweet wine suitable for desserts.

Pinot Gris, also known as Pinot Griglo and Tokay, is a heavy, full-bodied wine with spicy overtones.

Chenin Blanc can be very dry and very sweet. Interestingly, westerners prefer the dry versions, and easterners prefer the sweet.

Sémillon is a light wine, ranging from a dry to a semisweet. It is often blended with Cabernet Sauvignon.

Moscato Canelli/Muscat Canelli/Muscatel is a relatively new wine made in the U.S., ranging from very dry to sweet.

Pinot Blanc, a dry crisp wine, has slightly less flavor and intensity than its cousin, Chardonnay, and is quite inexpensive.

They're Not Wines, But...

Brandy is distilled mostly from white grapes, but is not a wine, as it contains more than 14% alcohol. When used in cooking, small amounts are generally used due to its potency. Brandy is best if aged at least 5 years. The finest of all Brandies is Cognac.

Sherry is a fortified wine which originated in Spain, and has a wide range of flavors and sweetnesses. Finos are dry and light, Manzanillas are very dry and very light with a hint of salt, Amontillados are a medium sherry with a nutty flavor and are darker, sweeter and softer than the Finos. Oloroso is the darkest, is more full flavored and is aged longer. It is also known as Cream Sherry or Golden Sherry.

Port is a sweet fortified wine, which is customarily served after a meal. The best Ports are labeled Late-Bottled Vintage Port, Single Vintage Port, and Tawny Port. Of Spanish origin, it has been made in the United States for more than 25 years.

Vermouth is a white wine that has been fortified and flavored with herbs and spices. It is available as Dry Vermouth, and Sweet Vermouth. Dry Vermouth is an aperitif or appetizer wine, and Sweet Vermouth is generally served with dessert. In cooking, Dry Vermouth is generally used in cooking mushrooms, chicken, pork and other light foods. Sweet Vermouth is used in cooking beef stews, marinading steaks and chops, etc.

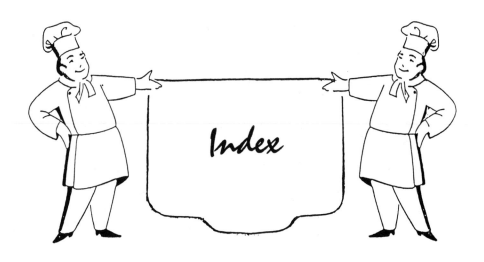

Index

Postscript

If your book, gift, or gourmet store does not have these books of ours, you may order them by phone, fax or mail.

"The Great Little Food With Wine Cookbook" (this book) . . . . $7.95 plus $2.00 S&H

"The California Wine Country Cookbook II", a collection of 172 favorite recipes by 102 chefs of "The California Wine Country". There's a section on cooking with wine, a brief history of wine in California . . . . . $12.95 plus $3.00 S&H

"The California Wine Country Herbs & Spices Cookbook", a collection of 188 recipes by 72 chefs, winemakers and wineries, featuring herbs and spices. Included in this book are recipes for making herbed oils and vinegars, and your own spice mixes . . . . $12.95 plus $3.00 S&H

"Cooking With Wine", a collection of 172 recipes for cooking with wine by 86 chefs, winemakers and wineries. Included, too, is a guide to using wine in your own recipes, and pairing wines with food . . . . $14.95 plus $3.00 S&H

To order, call toll free (800) 852-4890, Fax (707) 538-7371, or write to Hoffman Press, P.O. Box 2669, Santa Rosa, CA 95405. We accept MasterCard, VISA, American Express and Discover credit cards.

Your money back if you're not delighted!